WAR AND PEASE

WAR AND PEASE

Poems by Roland Pease

Zoland Editions

Published by Zoland Editions
Cambridge, Massachusetts
zolandeditions@gmail.com

ISBN: 979-8-218-46447-9

Copyright © 2024 by Roland Pease

Other books by Roland Pease:
Inside Out
Variety Store
The Trough
Roland Sez, etc.

Cover photograph by Roland Pease, taken at an anti-war march in Washington D.C. (1965)

Book design by Peter Paul Payack

For Lori, Anna and Nat
& to my good friends, my pillars.
And to all peacekeepers.

A Brief Introduction to War and Pease

For the most part I'll let my work speak for itself.

My title is a nod to Tolstoy, of course, but to all writers as well. As a grateful reader, I look to them for guidance, inspiration, knowledge and entertainment. The title is tongue-in cheek, as is much of my work. I view the world with love, horror & humor, and a profound belief that humans must get their act together before it is too late.

The poems are arranged alphabetically which spares me having to spend countless hours coming up with a haphazard flow of poems left and right.

— Roland Pease

"Only the dead have seen
the end of war."

— Plato

"You can no more win a war
than you can win an earthquake."

— Jeanette Rankin

"What you do makes a difference,
and you have to decide what kind of
difference you want to make."

— Jane Goodall

WAR AND PEASE

A Comic Episode

It had to do with working relations
gone amuck. Cleaning houses of in-
tangibles, non sequiturs sniffed out.
Various possibilities. Streamlined, we
tacked on a new list to adhere to when
going on the hunt. This took some time.
Home truths got us going, did they ever.
One practical joke produced belly laughs.
Uncommon and lowdown, we dressed as
if we were undershirts. We played the part,
throwing shade when we could, keeping our
cool, working for you hand and foot. Tally Ho.

A Feast for The Eyes

An ocean. Waves rolling in relentlessly. A thunderstorm was building with exceptional clouds moving by. A few gulls here and there. The boat on the horizon making its way elsewhere.

I couldn't have asked for more. Fascination in a sublime sky. Casual in an astounding way. Only nature has a need to be moving flat-out every singular moment of every solitary day.

A One-Way Day

My soul against your wall
leaving me no room at all.
Yesterday a one-way day

if ever I've seen one.
Fears flooding eyes,
spilling cries, hiding

beneath peculiar moods.
Silhouettes rounding the
corner, coming to a halt.

Stumbling blocks are
ripe all over the place,
making us sigh some.

The dearth of dreams trips us
up on sod of clumsy concerns
where nothing works as well

as it might. Moving on by.
Write well, feel well, look
well, be well, locate a view.

A Perfect Game

They are starting to notice.
In the heat of the moment

the pressure mounts.
Much comes to mind.

Every move you make
is under consideration.

Brains are
kicking in.

What have
we here?

Pray hard.
Play ball.

Smooth
operator.

Slow it
down.

Beside
myself.

Erase it
from

your
mind.

Power-
house.

Ruth-
less.

Suck
it up.

Pin it
down.

The hell
you say.

Aliens

> "They stood in the rain like farm animals."
> — *The Road,* Cormac McCarthy

Freaked at first,
I guessed they'd

be on the move soon,
knew we would cross

paths eventually.
They aren't about

to move yet & we
aren't either. I feel

like hollering, but
know that would

be useless. Must I
tear my hair out?

Mad dash? The die
is cast—we are on

call, as are they. If
only we knew what

to do next. We were
on our way to some

sort of party over at
Mel's. Cancel those

plans. All thumbs, as
that saying goes. Not

a clue what to do if
& when they move.

Is this some sort of initiation
I don't know anything about?

Asphyxiation

> "Death is a familiar thought, but when it
> visits me, I give it the back of my hand."
> — Ivan Turgenev

In the night like Zola.
Gone in the morning.

Fumes doing me in.
The enemy is silent,

sure as shit, creeps
in and does the job.

Life's over and done
for. Prepare yourself

sufficiently, be at the
real, right and ready.

Smoke stifles with
a steady insistence

that won't be denied.
Quite some adversary.

Such a way to go.
I guess there are

worse ways. I'm
not choosing this,

though, drifting
off as I am now,

alive as long
as I am able.

At the End Of The Day #2

Looking in the mirror
for signs of improve-
ment—not a chance.

Confidence is such a
relevant component.
Never forget it has

healing powers,
but don't mis-
lead yourself.

Be a realist at
all times; know
your every scar.

Hop to. Grab mind
over matter, and do
something about it.

Unwind: take time
to take a load off.
Remember to be.

Beat Me to The Punch

It comes with the territory. Such a blow to the head. Shake off
another one. Do unto others as they'd do unto you—in the ring
that just means bash away. Get to him if you're able before he gets
to you. It cannot be beat, this contest: as honest as the day
is long. I'll hand it to you if you can outsmart me, outbox me,
reduce me to tears. Ha! That will be the day. You might sneak
a punch in from time to time, but like the rest of the bunch you
are going down. Why it entertains me I'll never quite know why.

Belittled

Bothered beyond belief, we
watch the troops march by.

How are we to know the whole
truth of this miserable matter,

we who have no clout whatsoever?
Soldiers are being blamed for the

invasion, but many of us understand
there are powers behind their power.

These hamlets are being obliterated.
Grunts are doing what's been ordered.

Are humans so paltry, so eager to go
about their business blaming others

that they make the meek even weaker
than ever? Seems so. What many of us

desire is reasonable enough: wealth, harmony &
sex, love, food, health & pleasantries, intoxicants.

But our tactics are always killing us. How odd.
Murder is how we act out. One day this world

will be lost and we will moan, covered in decay,
in decadence. Peace is around the bend, but you

cannot get there. People belittle other people for fun
and games. Our planet remains on alert, in jeopardy.

Pray for all you are worth—we are the endangered.
The final chapter of the story has yet to be written.

Blows My Mind

> "After I sell all the cows, I keep going
> out to the pasture to look for them."
> — *Franny and Zooey,* J.D. Salinger

Making a go of it.
A business, after
all, farming is all
of that. Now I'm
left alone, ready
and willing to get
cracking, chickens
laugh at me, that
red rooster mocks
me out all day long.
This way, that way.
It blows my mind
how hard I work.
Don't mind if I do.

Cape Hatteras

It is where we contemplate
what amazes us, do or die.

Winds announce it first
then the gulls repeat it:

a message to those who
dare. Dunes and waves.

Instrumental factors
bring us face to face

with what is there. Always
tough to take, it's what we

have: such scary, inevitable truths.
Sounds grow louder, much bolder.

If there is a culprit it has no name
just an image of the vast unknown.

God only knows, and even then, there
is doubt about that. Nothing's certain.

Carrying On

> "Shared joy is a double joy;
> shared sorrow is half a sorrow."
> — Swedish proverb

Beyond belief
speaking his
fine head off
thinking out
loud he was
a reply wait-
ing to happen; and
we did respect him
for his hunger to be
out there & doing it.
Some are too silent
and secretive under-
neath, scary as the
night is slinky. This
man was mortal and
off the wall, very us,
expressing thoughts
so all up in our grills.
Presenting like a pro
like the best of us do
that hero is our hero.

Caution: Cattle Crossing #4

No news is greater news,
so they say. I say watch

out for nature every chance
you get. There is no defense

against an irate critter with
nothing superb up its sleeve.

Do not get sidetracked or you
just might end up a sore loser.

Leave it to me; leave it alone if
you know what is good for you.

I have been known to take one
on the chin, but I'd rather not.

The Farm was where I hung out
when I was feeling out of sorts.

Changed My Mind

I faced the facts
and they faced
me in the morn-
ing—full of them-
selves under their
breath. Pipe down,
I said, but they would
not. I let down my guard,
I thought it over, I got on
a raft, they thought me daft,
and I drifted and glided, then
returned and baffled everybody
by saying I now believed the opposite
of what I once did. I faced some ill will.

Church Club

> "Civilization will not attain
> perfection until the last stone
> from the last church
> falls on the last priest."
> — Emile Zola

My father states
Christian Soldiers
are on the push.

Ambitious men are
taking over. Godly
manipulators, the

scary kind, oh! My
father clues me in.
Religious wars are

common enough, we
know: bodies buried
throughout times. It

begins inside those
holy individuals who
have such initiatives.

Religion is where you
can crawl when skies
darken all around you

but do not tell me there
are any answers handy.
Revelations are too rare.

Confessions of The Donald

I have the key to the universe,
because you gave it to me, you
idiots. I plan to use it to the max.
Wouldn't you? I see my name on
everything, don't you? Me, Mine.
I am what you needed, a High &
Mighty He. Watch me take over.
Plain and simple strategy. Take.
There isn't anything I can't grab,
if you know what I mean. And I
am mean, the meaner the better.
They love it and plead for more.
I'm head over heels in love with
my reflection, my Hair of Hairs,
and even Melania believes I have
the best power & glory & money.
She cries her eyes out when I do
it to her, and though I do not do
it to her well anymore, I can do
it with gusto. Huge. And then I
tweet—I much prefer doing that.
I've got something going there.
I change every subject because I
can never remember what I just
said. Racist? Sexist? That is Me.
See people squirm. Scare them.
I've taken over. I must admit I
plan to take us all down soon.

I have no pit in my stomach.
We did my buddy Epstein in,
we could not let him testify,
as there was no other way to
silence him. Oh, the sex we had:
that young girly entertainment.
Vlad and I, and Un, are buddies.
We are so hot under our collars.
We are the architects of The End.
On my terms, baby, on my terms.

Council of War

Dead set against
peace at any cost.

Made a fuss about
it, splitting hairs &

delving into details
that seemed obscure

to all but the Generals.
I was worried to death

as I heard their arguments
verging on idiocy. I had no

vote as I was only on hand
to take notes and hand out

sugar cookies & whisky &
such. War was in the offing.

Crammed with Soak

Heard some crack pot
utter: How Art Thou?

We were on Lexington Avenue.
Quite a joke-storm was brewing.

What a tempest hit us recently
but we recovered nicely in time

to get on with our lives. Drenched,
we were a little under the weather.

Some states announce themselves.
Everything we wore was saturated.

We huddled closer and vied for the
warmth we could locate in corners.

Eat your thoughts, I was told twice, as I
said something about sunny skies being

long gone and hard to find. A wiry cop was
ready to slap me in the slammer but I made

myself scarce so he wandered off muttering.
We frittered away the days during the damp

cramped with soak and little else, seeking some
kind of protection, kindness, shelter and serenity.

It is times like these that fry one's soul, and yet what else are we supposed to do with our lives?

Comes a time when we either put up or shut up. Wet is what can be, and we better just accept it.

Dark dank halls lead and we frequently follow. The drip, drip, drip of consequence beckons us.

Dentist Session

I was told to relax my cheeks.
I was told my tongue was too
large for my mouth. I was told
I had a superb supply of saliva.

Our chatter was not far-reaching.
The doctor had amazing earlobes.
I looked out the window at clouds.
I played it safe and kept quite quiet.

Down and Dirty and Then Some

Grab your shillelagh. Do battle
with those warriors you must do
battle with. Similar sorts. They're
up to no good and neither are you.
Somewhat old school, often peckish,
we're dead wrong. Rub them out now
or break bread with them once wounds
have healed. Snatch victory from the jaws
of defeat or go down in infamy as a rotter.
This is not what I signed up for, not at all.

Egads

Hornswoggle slipped
out of my lips today
at lunch and I was
looked at funny
not for the first
time either. I
followed up
with pooh-
pooh, too.
Giddy-up.
I daresay.
Verily.
Egads.
Pithy.
Daft.
Afar.
Mar.

Every Word I Voice Is One Less Word I Write

You will not catch me alert
gathered in a boardroom as

a member of a brain trust
checking charts for growth,

assessing accountabilities.
With scoundrels swindling

each other as often as possible
I'm more likely to be deep in a

forest, shadowboxing in the earliest
morning sunshine, locating my way,

celebrating leaves on trees, breezes,
buds, birds, et cetera. Finding exact

words on the tip of my tongue is a day
well spent in my opinion. If I can get it

down on the page, so much the better. Yet
evaporation is part of the process and some

of the best ideas fly far away like with dreams.
I must often refuse to speak or answer the door

or phone because I will lose something in the
process. I make friends with the individuals I

have learned to love; they comprehend my silences.
Everything will come out in the wash, even words

that I once wanted to use, forgot, and knew would
return if given half a chance. I'm hunting for them.

Eye to Eye

We are bent on doing each other in, not to the death but close enough. Clobber him, slobber on him, do what you can to slay his spirits, get him so down he can't look up. To top things off, I will get better as the fight goes on so quit now sucker or else.

Fact #9

> "Cows are amongst the gentlest
> of breathing creatures."
> — Thomas De Quincy

I'll see to it as soon
as I possibly can. If
what you say is true,
my cows are in your
field eating your crops.
That must be stopped, I
agree. Let me finish this
poem first and then I will
go get my Daisy and Maisy
and bring them on home. I
have always liked their spunk.
You could say they are playing
the field, or not. You are serious,
and so shall I be right about now.
A shame you do not see it my way.
This poem must be abandoned now.
I won't belabor the point, but bovines
have a place in my heart that you never
will. Something about their aim is truer.

Fact #36

My moat is grimy, slimy, and full of creatures you do not want to mess with. They possess rows of teeth that are sharp & ready. Loathsome chums. I'm reduced to this. Unseemly at best. In fact, these giant beasts are trained to take it all in. If you want to visit me, do call ahead. No room for error. Never been better.

Fact #44

I was once told
I was high-strung.

I was once labeled
demure. Cut the shit.

Obsequious. I beg to differ.
Enlightened. No, not yet. I

am not the man you think I am, and
I may not be who I think I am either.

Fog Horn

There is something out there.
They know it. Collisions are
inevitable. Prepare if you can.
Beware and then: ahoy. Swells
are from some recent hurricane.

Water, being what it is in all its
forms, is wild until tamed. I'll
never understand fish, and I'm
working on the nature of man.
That horn is regular and noisy.

The day will end up one way or
another. I do not know praying.
I'm counting on the luck I hope
I'm due today and in the future.
A fog horn indicates something.

Found Poem

Sixty "saltwater brothers," who years ago clung to hope as
the torpedoed cruiser Indianapolis sank in the South Pacific,
gathered yesterday for the launching of their ship's namesake,
a high-speed nuclear attack submarine.

The survivors, whose doomed World War Two vessel had just
delivered parts of the atomic bomb that was to level Hiroshima
one week later, watched as the new 360-foot Indianapolis submarine
slid into the Thames River.

"We've got a bond that no one else has got. We are all saltwater
brothers," said one of the survivors.

Only 316 of the 1192 men who abandoned the stricken Indianapolis
lived through the five-day ordeal of clinging to whatever else would
keep them afloat in shark-infested waters under searing sunlight.

No SOS was sent because of the Indianapolis's secret atomic mission.
The clandestine delivery was to the island of Tinian. The vessel was
torpedoed July 30, 1945.

Getting Gypped

Never going
there again.

I saw it coming on
but he was way too

fast for the likes of me.
I did my damnedest to

control my temper
after the fact. Did

not go back and lay
into him. Proof was

gone. I simmered
& learned a lesson

though I'm not sure
I could articulate it

better than I already
have. Advance along.

Over my head back then.
No harm done in the end.

Misfits keep us guessing
along our paths to home.

Gut check is the buzzword.
It instantly comes to mind.

Ghosts

> "Yes, there's something
> the dead are keeping back."
> — *The Witch of Coos,* Robert Frost

They are all about
our living rooms—

in our very beds,
attics and cellars

sliding along
our corridors

like aliens from far-outer
space. Floorboards creak.

Ghosts attract attention
and dogs do bark. Spirits

are more than merely a
notion, invisible visions.

We end up doing exactly what
they command us to do. They

order us around, though we
can't comprehend that—we

do what we do. A silence
profoundly surrounds us.

We are in awe of them.
They want to take over,

sharing our precious air,
but never in our lifetime.

Give It a Go

Gone in a flash.
Better you than
me, a sail in the
sea, in troubled
waters, a squall.
Dire warnings in
among so much,
sailors and such.
Lifeboats afloat.
A skeleton crew.
No bigwigs about.
No laps of luxury.
It serves us right.
Take it or leave it.

Good Luck Ambassador

"The dead are nowhere and everywhere."
— *The Proof,* Agota Kristof

I believe his name was Quigley
and he came from a block over.

He was a smooth talker and I
rather respected him at first.

Then he wore out his welcome,
his politics began to show and

they stunk up the joint. He got
under my skin in the worst way.

I ducked out on one conversation
by saying my Auntie Mue needed

to see me. She'd died decades ago
but I didn't think she'd mind. She

would probably smile one of those
swell smiles of hers. I rest my case.

Hark!

A knocking on the door in
the middle of the night had

me on edge right off the bat.
I moved quietly and quickly

to my upstairs window, then
looked at the stranger below.

I know it is risky to say hello
but I said hello, who are you?

Things were best left just the way
they were, beyond the unthinkable.

Bother has our names on it all too frequently.
Panic could have set in but I went back to bed.

I have

so much I
want to do

so much I
want to say

before I exit
one day from

this earth of
ours. Here

is hoping I have
an extended stay

then I can state what
I have to in a manner

that matters to others
as well as to myself. I

have a need, we all do,
to find more meanings.

Here is to doing what I know
I can do if given enough time.

I'm about to

make the most of it;

shape up or ship out;

leave these premises;

hand in my dance card;

rejoice; get cracking;

go around the bend;

give fair warning;

do due diligence;

lose track of time;

create a side hustle;

lie through my teeth;

give fair warning;

take my tug to sea;

streamline my life;

be on the look-out;

kiss and hug my wife;

be as happy as can be;

Play The Jazz Messengers;

say Jumping Jehoshaphat;

cross my heart & hope to die;

tie up loose ends;

know my own mind;

play practical jokes;

make ends meet;

take it from here;

read my fortune;

vent my wrath;

blow my top;

storm off;

go sideways;

take a breather;

take a midnight run;

fight fire with fire;

walk a picket line;

keep my mouth shut;

take things in stride;

swig and swallow;

thumb my nose;

tell a white lie;

laugh to myself;

blow my stack;

take no notice;

blow him off;

have you on;

forget not;

carry on;

brood;

jeer;

peer;

pee.

Nonsense

That's nonsense
I was informed
but I knew that
was not at all
true. Perish
the thought.
Play the field.
Run for cover.
Eat your words.
Eat eclairs. Eat
shit. Eat ill will.
Eat high spirits.
Eat your vermin.
Eat your loony bin.

On the Down-Low

Out and out war
was being waged
under cover of dark:

inside out, worn down,
blood lust hunkering in
a shed near the edge of

slim hopes; battering rams,
mortars, cannons & drones;
hotheads, hardships, hearsay.

Pitchfork Heaven

A hands-on approach
works every time, as
far as I know. "Rouse
the Cows" is heard on
a need to hear basis. I,
for one, enjoy the work
that is done around here.
Do not jump to conclusions.
Chickens are underfoot and
creep me out from time to time,
but you've got to admit they are
an original thought, so very them.
I pay attention to all of the details.
Pigs generally do their own thing.
Other than that, if memory serves,
much is straight forward—unless
Frank comes around, and then when
that happens his dog Franklin comes
too, and he messes around some. I've
been known to pick up this pitchfork
and threaten to poke his sorry ass, but
I don't. Like I say all takes care of itself.

Push Comes to Shove

For Denise Levertov

Right in Harvard Square.
One more demonstration

against an immoral war in Viet
Nam. That teargas. Billy Clubs.

Being chased down Mass Ave.
Those were the days, not to be

confused with the good old days.
Sex, drugs and rock 'n roll were

around, but protests against an
idiotic, cruel, wasteful war were

a way we had to go. Risking injuries.
We'll never forget nor should we ever.

We'd get to the bottom of it, we believed, young, idealistic as we were.

Don't mess with me, we said, facing
the grim pigs in their suits of armor.

On that big stage, fighting for other lives,
and ours as well, flying a flag of freedom.

Put Up Your Dukes

In saying so a fight was on.
There was no turning back.

No one victory could be big
enough to excuse the blows

that would define that need
to succeed. In landing those

punches, this fighter felt grand, knew
he could topple barns if he wished to.

His power was that stupendous
in his heart, in his imagination.

Opponents were free to test his skills.
He welcomed their advances. When

fights were over he felt such remorse.
He wanted something to laugh about.

He played Chaplin films over &
over. The Marx Brothers as well.

The urge to fight puzzled him some but he never
questioned it for long; it was what he did so well.

Question(?) Museum

Where is it?
Why is that?

Who are you? Who
is too sick at heart?

Why are gumshoes
gathered outside?

What could be in those
pigeonholes of yours?

What is the meaning
of your shady dealings?

Why is their Lost and
Found full of answers?

Does it have to be a me-me-
me world every single day?

Did you turn your back
on me for a good reason?

Do we really have to go back
to the drawing board again?

Over my dead body is not
a question but an answer

so why are you looking at
me funny & why are there

no doors in or doors out of this
museum—no windows as well?

Can unforced errors be the key
to what we know must be true?

Rocking the Boat

In Southie I knew
I was not where I
should be. I was
stalked and
walked fast

turned a corner
ducking into
a doorway.
Hiding out.
He went by.

I felt like I should
have followed him,
giving him a lesson
he'd never forget, but
logic got the best of me

that uncomfortable day.
I have not been back to
Southie since. No need to.
Finding my pleasures elsewhere.
Finding my terrors elsewhere, too.

Roland Sez #131

For My Two

Marchin' as to war
against all combat.

April 29th NYC,
20th & Broadway

to Foley Square.
Turbulent times.

Bush bumbles,
scaring us to

death. Iraq
and Katrina.

Hundreds of
thousands

protest. Me
and my two,

too. I am proud
of them, of their

earnest outrage.
Carrying signs.

All eyes and ears
being counted. My

feet hurt, being on
them for five hours

wasn't good for
my neuropathy,

but the show must go
on. One must be heard,

seen, march & march
more. Never ending. In

Chinatown, we searched
for taxicabs; no luck until

some luck. We made it back
uptown in time to see dear

old Dad for dinner at The Mark.
Quite a day in every way. Being

alive. Standing for what one
believes in. Prepared to fight.

Dad said he fought in WWII
for over one hundred years.

He was starting to go around
the bend, the ancient soldier.

I will never remain silent and I insist
on teaching that to mine, reminding

them that all things are political,
and: don't ever lapse into apathy.

Roland Sez #133

I hope this finds you fine.
Recently I saw you slink,

which means you slunk
past me on the boulevard.

What was that about?
I might have done the

same if given
half a chance.

We haven't liked each
other for many years,

but I still do not wish you
harm. Thanks for slinking.

No question about it—as
human as human can be.

Long time no see. Hoping it
happens again: never seeing

you, as the case may be. That
is the way it goes now & then.

Roland Sez #178 Haiku

Mother's 102nd.
Died 78 years ago.
How I miss her so!

Roland Sez #204

The road to ruin runs
right past our houses.

We are onlookers, are
do-gooders, are savvy,

and longshoremen, too;
olde school, sometimes,

free spirits on occasion;
we know crapola when

we come across it, and
we come across it on a

regular basis. Stooges
hold the reins much of

the time; allies of ours,
too. A mixed bag. Mine

eyes have seen the terrors
of the coming of the horde.

I couldn't have said it any
better. God made me do it.

Being real right now, blunt
perhaps, but spot on again.

Having the time of my life.
How about you? Why not?

Roland Sez #224

Such a sing-song sound.
Lulled to sleep on a wave.

Unpleasantness at bay—
for another day it seems.

Fingers crossed for more
of the same. A fluke, sure,

finding ourselves on such
an adventure, to be here;

the question: is there a
sequel? That's what we

want to know. I have a
sneaking suspicion: no.

Roland Sez #253

What does fail-safe
mean to you? I once
read a novel with that
title, not bad, made into
a movie, too, I do believe. It
came into my life once more
today when I received a piece
of mail addressed to me care of
Fail-Safe. That leaves me puzzled
and uncomfortable. There is nobody
I can turn to for any advice. Inside the
envelope is this following message, "To
you sir, learn the hard way. All you do is a
little suspect, and it remains to be seen if you
can prove otherwise. We are watching your every
move. You're known to us as Fail-Safe. It's kind of
a joke, but not really. Wise-up. You haven't been your-
self recently. Talk to your better half and see if you can
improve things. We won't take no for an answer, and you
know we mean business. We will see you on the other side."
Seems to me it's a crank doing their best to cause me grief. I
reject manuscripts daily, and some odd writer is probably out
to get me. With words. A kook. A freak. A good for nothing. It re-
mains to be seen if anything comes of this. The police would only
laugh, place the mail in a folder, and file it under something or other.
I won't even talk to my wife about it. I'm telling you just in case anything
happens. Hardy har-har. Quite a joke, Biff. Are you up to no good again?

Roland Sez #256

Now, where were we?
Ah, yes, under the wire
just in the nick of time.

Imagine this: me and my
buddies, all incognito, doing
our best to keep it on the Q.T.,

marching together in solidarity, past
the sentries in their stare-down mode.
They could not see us for who we were.

If ever I was to feel nervous that would
have been the time, but I was as cool as
a cucumber. There is something terribly

exciting about doing what you can
to serve that cause you know is
right and well worth dying for.

Roland Sez #273

"There are causes worth dying for,
but none worth killing for."
— Albert Camus

Alive and kicking.
The here and now.

Crimes of passion
are all around us.

Be vigilant at all
times or else. We

know the drill. If
we let down our

guard, we will be-
come one of them.

Decide who you'll
defend and make

a promise out of it.
All the better for it.

Roland Sez #329

"Zat so."
— B. Traven

Leave no stone unturned. A voice in my nut demands this of me. I'm not happy with this whatsoever: who can speak to me like that?

I will have to walk out the door right about now and insist that that voice shut the hell up. I'm demanding that demand take a hike.

Roland Sez #389

The tempo was like you would not believe.
Not bad for old-timers. Stoics. A few were
mouthing off that day, but the snoops were

shut-in, shut-up. The fortress was not far away,
and we were hell-bent-for-leather to get there
before our energies burnt out. We had to take

a break to down our 5-hour energy drinks, and
that put something dreadful in us. Some misfit
said, "I want to wring your neck," but other than

that, the invasion went as well as it could have—
and yet the mighty stronghold was deserted with
a notice on the door saying, "tough luck, lug-nuts."

We went in and all around and we found nothing
to our liking, but we told the folks back home we
had driven the enemy away, so it was a great day.

Roland Sez #393

Getting to the bottom of it, I'm vexed.
Flights of fancy were flying overhead.

That call was a mistake in my mind.
High crimes & misdemeanors were

on display, were cloaked as well off,
were in lock-step, so help us, oh God.

Wrestling with our consciousnesses, we
buckled down yet again, so bleary-eyed.

All in all, nothing could be truer; we felt
such pain, we felt for each other, we felt.

Roland Sez #394

For Paul Auster

8/20: Vietnam War Lottery: #344.
How lucky could I get? No worries.

But the crap I had to deal with before-
hand could have sunk a tug. Numerous

trips to the Boston Army base, hanging
out in my skivvies with hundreds of other

men. Missile meat. Never ready to fight.
The absurdities & horrors of what gives.

I had something else in mind: Peace, Love
and Understanding. Who are you to talk?

Tough minded in the long run, fighting
against a war with every fiber of myself,

facing facts and not facing facts, either,
stalling, begging off, being a fortunate.

Under the circumstances, all considering,
I did fine for myself, thank you very much.

Roland Sez #443

The night watchman has
his eyes on me. He sees
me coming and going
and I see him see me.
We make quite a pair.
We need each other.
I circle back around.
He has a right to be
suspicious. I am to
scout out all that I
know is there, as
well as all I don't
know is there. If
my disguise isn't
working, my air
of nonchalance
is. Watchman
doesn't know
what to do
with me:
he sees
me see
him,
yes,
no.

Roland Sez #452

Do not cast a blind eye on
what's going on nowadays.

Sharpen your ears. I am at the
very end of my rope, as Trump

performs treacherous acts of
deception that are villainous.

People treat him like some reality
show. No. No. No. Too many lives

are at stake. Now's not the time to
let up. Not whatsoever. Shout out.

Get him by any means possible.
Make a stir, for crying out loud,

we're being ripped off, and don't
we just know it. Bring him down!

Rules of Engagement

> "I'm not God but I'm
> something similar."
> — Roberto Duran

Fighting tooth and nail,
I see nothing but flesh.
No easy way out what-
so-ever. Truth be told,

I have my eye on you until I
do not have to anymore. If I
knock you out, as I'm about to
do, the chapter will be written.

Running Scared

Poetry matters
no matter what
some say. And
it surely can be
earth shattering.
Vibrant verse is
troublemaking.
Don't disappoint.
Animate arousal.
Revise until your
eyes cry out for a
chance to rest. I
know you have a
true doubt or two,
but keep on writing.
Hash it out between
now, then & never. Some
readers might run scared,
because they do not want
to be hit between the eyes.

Suicide Letter

Out of the blue.
Oh, brother, oh

sister, oh no, not
again. A betrayal

of trust. Of every
little thing. All for

nothing—in harm's
way one more time.

You'll catch your
death of defeat.

My heart goes out
to you, of course,

but I thought we
were past all that.

Received this letter
on an ordinary day.

Swim

Writing in my sleep.
Splashing upstream,

I continue to make every
effort I can to reach those

big goals I set out for myself.
Out of breath. Out of options.

I am having at it again. I insist
on having no spectators. Why

bother? Keeping myself company
without those shadows of a doubt.

Nonstop water keeps things fluid,
this & that, resistance all the way.

The Good Humor Man

No slouch, he.
His jibes were
New Jerseyish

with a bit of bite.
I learned the lingo,
but he was a master.

Take away that laughter
and the words would stick
it to you. Better learn to parry.

The Hope

It is in me still
refusing to die.

I may be ill, I
may hurt hard,

but I've in no way
given up the ghost,

nor do I plan to.
That is my vow

on this day in deepest
December, shady with

chilly and somber news.
I look to spring training.

I may even believe in life after
death, if you can believe that. I

entertain notions, yet remain one
logical individual. Trust me now.

I utilize my language for a living.
Knowledge often comes knocking.

I am doing more than killing time
as storm clouds swirl so overhead.

Everybody under our star remains
quite quizzical, busy beyond belief.

The Wind (1/12/2020)

For Greta

It came barreling across the city,
unnatural in its insistence, new
to us now that climate change
is a thing, a dangerous thing:
ferocious, fouling up our
ways of thinking about
ourselves, our world.
How have we acted
to produce this,
these spasms?
We've done it.
More in store.
Blundered.
Our failure
to act be-
fore now.
Hurry up.
We lost it.
Our stain.
Deceitful.
Wake up.
Wise up
every-
one.
Me.
Us.

Thems the Breaks

> "No one was paying any
> attention to the sky."
> — *Wise Blood,* Flannery O'Connor

Tougher Troopers
were memorizing
infiltration tactics.

I was the sergeant
in charge of it all,
and I felt like go-

ing very far away.
Honing our skills.
Hesitant, brooding.

And what was the
choice: to die or kill?
What a rule of thumb

to follow on a Sunday.
Yearning for much more.
Half the troops had the trots.

They

Some of them swipe
identities right off
faces, trade them
with sinister sorts.
That evil business.
Perish the thought.
Eyes may be on you
as we speak. En garde.
Know what's going on
around you at all times.
With rare character being
developed these days, what
is, is stolen like currency. Our
culture has come to this, and if
you aren't careful you too will
be on that fast track to oblivion.
Take precautions. Never let your
true self be seen in public places. If
you do, you will suffer consequences.

Trapdoor

> "Turn need inside out."
> — *God's Pauper,* Nikos Kazantzakis

I expected to be horrified.
I expected to be stricken.
I was enchanted instead.
I caught up with myself.
An urgency in decency
surrounded me. I left
bothers far behind.
I became renewed.

Unearth

"I bleat and bray my protests."
— Joel Cohen

At your own peril,
ask questions, sit
tight no more, be
active, not reactive,
assist others in need.
Our hearts are heavy.
Bark at all prejudice.
Take truth serum &
spit out facts to power.
Not out of the question.
Then obliterate idiocies.
We'll fucking overcome.

Uneasy #2

> "While there is a lower class, I am in it, while there is a criminal element, I am of it, and while there is a soul in prison, I am not free."
> — Eugene Debs

Cut to the quick. I'll maintain my position; I never waiver; I'll stick to my ideals; all my battles have been waged with all my heart and soul. Disquiet is how I feel most of the time. All's not how it should be. People suffer. What people will think is too often what is thought; I don't. Think twice before calling out my name in vain. I don't mince words.

Up Yours

Don't tell me what to do if you don't understand
what kind of person I am and what I am capable
of doing: when I hear idiots mouthing off, I start
to sharpen my skills, get my jab ready, go on the
offensive. Yes, I will pick my moments, counter-
punch and utilize my foot speed—do not mess
with me. Just because I look nice doesn't mean
I can't roll the dice, beat you at your own game.
I'd caution you to stay on my right side, or you
will be paying the price. I'm no Mister Nice Guy.
Years in the trenches have taught me how; I have
abilities you can only guess at in your nightmares.
Treat me right: I'll be your friend forever and ever.
And if you do not: I will be what you fear the most.

Wall of Green

Never rigid, the breeze
has its way with leaves.

There's no pinning it up.
Vermont's free spirits. I

am in awe of the silence
sometimes, the rustling.

I will stare and listen as
long as I'm ever able to.

War

It'll get you every time.
You march and march

some more. All strife
happens when peace

is taken for granted. Nobody
quarrels when peace breaks

out. Going off to war—there
is nothing like it, ones' worst

dreams. Killing humans to get
what you crave is a cruel crime,

is a reality unlike any other. It
is morbid to dwell on it for long,

but ignorant to ignore it forever.
War won't get us what we need.

Someday, someone bright enough
might get it right, do anything else.

We are nobody's fools: all of us are so
aware of what waits for us in the end,

but Denial is our middle name, and we
go on being beasts, trudging off to war.

War and Pease #2

One tough nut to crack
& whoever wanted to?

Ever-present. Piggyback
on pugilists of yore. I vie

for the space nearby, and will
box for the right to say mine.

War Machine

> "Maybe there's a God above
> But all I've ever learned from love
> Was how to shoot somebody who outdrew ya
> And it's not a cry you hear at night
> It's not somebody who has seen the light
> It's a cold and broken Hallelujah."
> — Leonard Cohen / Jeff Buckley

Dirty pool
performed.

It wasn't funny.
Not a single bit.

We lost our heads.
I beg your pardon.

Bodies were those
victims in the end.

Nolo contendere.
Bedlam prevailed.

Ill-at-ease leaders were
often guilty as charged

and the weaponry was
churned out like candy.

Money was being spent—
your dumb dime & mine.

Evangelists were emphatic,
chain-smoking: Hallelujah.

You Are the Best

For Lori

You are the best,
she declares, but

I disagree; I'm not
all I'm cracked up

to be. Too grouchy
at times, bellowing

curses when I stub
my toe, break a dish:

"GODDAMNIT." I have
been known to get up

in the hour of the wolf
and need to get to the

emergency ward: I cannot
breath; acute pains in my

pancreas. You are
the best, my dear,

she says once more.
I'm convinced she is.

You Have to Hope

"A swollen cloud a curving shadow
ripples light on the lumpy hill
Maybe so."
— Philip Whalen

I ran like hell on location
knowing it was Destiny
that could kill me there.

I picked up speed and
passed someone else
who could now be the

one in jeopardy. Never
one to take things easy,
I was on edge the rest of

my life. Thanks a bunch.
I have to think things can
improve. It's the way I am.

Young Polly

She never grew older,
never had a chance to,
is always young, always,
always dead, never alive for
long; long enough, though, to
have two children, one of them
me, two offspring who are twice
as old as Polly was the moment
she died more than seventy years
ago. It makes me wonder much of
the time—who could she have become?
Who would I have been under her influence?
Could her daughter have had an easier existence?
Polly: a woman who would have made a difference.

Roland Pease founded Zoland Books in Cambridge, Massachusetts with his wife, Lori. He was the publisher and editor there for fifteen years before becoming the fiction and poetry editor at Steerforth Press, in Hanover, New Hampshire. He was an editor at Phone-A-Poem, and also the publisher and editor of *Zoland Poetry, an Annual of Poems, Translation and Interviews.* He has had poems published in *The Paris Review, The Boston Globe, The New York Times, Let the Bucket Down, Can We Have Our Ball Back,* and other publications.

www.ingramcontent.com/pod-product-compliance
Lightning Source LLC
Chambersburg PA
CBHW051658040426
42446CB00009B/1199